MY LIFE ASLEEP

My Life Asleep

Jo Shapcott

Oxford   New York
OXFORD UNIVERSITY PRESS
1998

821. 91 SHA

92158

Oxford University Press, Great Clarendon Street, Oxford OX2 6DP
Oxford New York
Athens Auckland Bangkok Bogotá Buenos Aires Calcutta
Cape Town Chennai Dar es Salaam Delhi Florence Hong Kong Istanbul
Karachi Kuala Lumpur Madrid Melbourne Mexico City Mumbai
Nairobi Paris São Paulo Singapore Taipei Tokyo Toronto Warsaw
and associated companies in Berlin Ibadan

Oxford is a registered trade mark of Oxford University Press

First published in Oxford Poets
as an Oxford University Press paperback 1998

British Library Cataloguing in Publication Data
Data available

Library of Congress Cataloging in Publication Data
Shapcott, Jo, 1953–
My life asleep / Jo Shapcott.
I. Title.
PR6069.H288M9   1998   821'.914—dc21   98-22117

ISBN 0–19–288103–5

1 3 5 7 9 10 8 6 4 2

Typeset by George Hammond Design
Printed in Great Britain by
Athenæum Press Ltd.
Gateshead, Tyne and Wear

Acknowledgements

Poems in this collection have appeared in the following magazines, newspapers, and anthologies: *Atlanta Review, The Devil, The Independent, Klaonica* (Bloodaxe Books, 1993), *New Writing Three* (British Council/Minerva, 1994), *New Writing Five* (British Council/Vintage, 1996), *Penguin Modern Poets* 12, *Poetry Review, Poetry Wales, Sixty Women Poets* (Bloodaxe Books, 1993), *Verse*; and in the pamphlet *Motherland* (Gwaithel and Gilwern, 1996). Some of the poems were commissioned by the South Bank Centre's Literature Department and National Touring Exhibitions, and others by the Association of British Orchestras together with British Telecommunications plc for Stephen Montague's composition, *The Creatures Indoors.* 'Delectable Creatures' was commissioned by the Blue Nose Poets for their Freud evening.

Warm thanks to The Society of Authors and to the Arts Council of England for their support during the writing of this book.

The title of the poem 'Delectable Creatures' is from W. H. Auden's poem 'In Memory of Sigmund Freud'; I'm indebted to Wendy Wheeler for her account of her dream. The first three lines of 'Brünhilde' are a fragment of Auden's conversation as quoted in *The Table Talk of W. H. Auden*, Alan Ansen, edited by Nicholas Jenkins, Faber & Faber, 1991. For 'Mandrake Pie' I am indebted to *The Joy of Cooking* for the history of pie-making. In 'Professional Mourner' I am indebted to *Dancing on the Grave: Encounters with Death*, Nigel Barley, Abacus, 1997. 'Noah's Dove' was written together with Arie van den Berg.

The fifteen versions taken from Rilke's *Les Roses* (originally 27 poems) follow Rilke's numbering, rather than a new consecutive one.

Contents

What are all those
fuzzy-looking things out there?
                    —William Carlos Williams

Thetis

No man can frighten me. Watch as I stretch
my limbs for the transformation, I'm laughing
to feel the surge of other shapes beneath my skin.
It's like this: here comes the full thrill of my art
as the picture of a variegated
lizard insinuates itself into my mind.
I extend my neck, lengthen fingers, push
down toes to find the form. My back begins
to undulate, the skin to gleam. I think
my soul has slithered with me into this
shape as real as the little, long tongue in my mouth,
as the sun on my back, as the skill in absolute stillness.
My name is Thetis Creatrix and you,
voyeur, if you looked a little closer, would see
the next ripples spread up my bloody tail, to bloom
through my spine as the bark begins to harden
over my trunk. Already I'm so much the oak
I lean everything towards the black oxygen
in the black air, I process delicious gases
through my personal chemistry, suck moisture
from the earth to a pulse so slow you can't detect it.
Next tigress. Low tremendous purrs start at the pit
of my stomach, I'm curving through long grass,
all sinew, in a body where tension
is the special joy and where the half-second
before a leap tells it all. Put out a paw
to dab a stone, an ant, a dead lamb. Life,
my life, is all play even up to the moment
when I'm tripped up, thrown down, bound,
raped until I bleed from my eyes,
beaten out of shape and forced to bring forth War.

*Thetis was a sea goddess who had the marvellous ability to change her shape.
Peleus was taught by Proteus the way to overcome her: to bind her and hold on
tightly whatever shape she took. The result of this forced union was Achilles.*

1

The Swallows Move In

You, with the new haircut, steadily
scrape birdshit from the sink and from
the rusty washing machine, because
swallows are nesting in your outhouse

and mustn't be disturbed. Didn't you notice
lightning shake the wires where the birds
perch at dusk? While you scrub the smelly drainer
and prod at dung in the bowl, the city shakes

with news from Europe, with news of the minister
and the actress, with news of the prince
and the married woman. Houses subside
all over London, and a taxi-driver swore

he'd seen medieval apprentices skating
on frozen Moorfields with bones of animals
tied to their shoes to swirl them across the ice.
You patiently lay old papers for protection

across the lawnmower and the bicycle,
the sink and the sad spin-dryer. A crumb
of shit is in your eye but you try to wink
back at the newspaper photographs of ministers,

married women, murdered women, refugees,
the mauled and mutilated of the world,
the weeping dead themselves, photographs
which make you wonder how a person

could look at that and not die of shame,
the same photos you are spreading
with care against the dirt of swallows who play
and swoop at midges in the light summer air.

War and Peace

The woods of Normandy are hot with stars
underfoot, resistance and memory.
It's the Queen's birthday and we know the stars
are flowers in reality because
today flowers are everywhere for her.
Yellow smoke hangs over the bridge
at Mostar and someone has taken
huge bites out of the town, chewed up
apartment blocks. Yes, it's peacetime.
Grab your shopping trolley at Tesco's
and read the sign: *DO NOT HESITATE*

WHEN PASSING THROUGH THIS GATE
and you don't, you don't hesitate
knowing you're about to buy a world
in the supermarket someone else
lost recently. Peacetime. Here is Mostar
still dressed in yellow smoke. The Queen
marks her anniversary by doing a bungee jump
at Crystal Palace, a two-hundred feet plunge,
in full regalia. She yo-yos up and down
as her tiara crashes to the ground.
Meanwhile, behind the roof of the château

yellow clouds rise where windows, even frames
blow out; the works of art are moved elsewhere.
The problem is not living together, pulling together,
the problem is dying. A little boat
leaves the bridge at Mostar and shudders
towards the white mists of Niagara,
whose plunge and roar is thrilling all the tourists.
Peace. The engines grind against the undertow
as the captain takes us as far into the mist
and thunder as he thinks we dare to go.

3

'Delectable Creatures'

You won't remember, but it was
October and the street trees
still coloured like rude bouquets.
I had some rare walks by the river,
the weak sun loose on the water
and the light so washed out and lovely
it would make you cry if you weren't
completely alert. Every step I took
they were uncovering something: people
sleeping under cardboard, a lost riverboat
marooned on a freak low tide, the buried flotsam
which made metal detectors buzz, theatres
with resonant names: the Rose, the Globe.

And I was carrying a torch for someone
to the point of hallucination:
we rolled in flames through seven fields, the burning
so thorough I longed to be shocked by water,
a faceful of anything, even the smelly Thames.

And I remember the press full of doctors,
of inventions; a herringbone fragment
of DNA to fool a virus, a wisp
of vitamin to lock on to inner decay
and knock it dead for good. We were
saving vouchers, too, for air miles.

There was, O yes, the morning I woke up
to see an open book, drying on the drainer.
Dimly reconstructing the night before
I remembered dropping off, head on the desk,
getting up moments later, to select the book
with extra-exquisite care from any old shelf.
I slowly chose a page, spread it with jam
and butter, and tried to stuff it down my mouth.
It was, of course, Freud's *Jokes and the Unconscious.*
I must have tried to wash it like a tea plate,
stacked it, then put myself into my bed.

I think the explanation could be this:
that in the light, the river was sometimes pink,
and St Paul's was pink, and even Lloyds
in the distance was pink, as I crossed Waterloo Bridge
with a purchase under my arm, some piece
of frou frou or a novel to bring me back
from the seven fields, back to the river-mist
which must once have been river water, back
to breathing mist so deeply I could feel
each droplet hit my diaphragm like shot.

Quark

'Transcendental,' said the technician,
'to stumble on a quark that talks back.
I will become a mystagogue, initiate
punters into the wonder of it for cash.'
'Bollocks,' said the quark, from its aluminium
nacelle. 'I don't need no dodgy
crypto-human strategising my future.
Gonna down-size under the cocoplum
or champak, drink blue marimbas into
the sunset, and play with speaking quarklike
while I beflower the passing gravitons.'

The Alchemist

I've waited my whole life for these few atoms
to swim, synchronised, into tetrahedra
(that's diamonds to you, sunshine, crystal gold).
But it all goes pear-shaped or, at least, cuboid,
so I end up with pyrites or galenae
or magnificent prisms of boring, boring quartz.
But you, my auriferous lovely, have just to breathe
and mica condenses in the very air.
I'm the acolyte of your reticulations,
a zealot for your mineral ideology.

My Life Asleep

Everything is loud: the rasp of bed-sheets,
clamour of hair-tangles, clink of teeth.
Small sweat takes up residence in each crease
of the body, but breathing's even, herself warm,
room safe as a London room can be.
The tube rumbles only metres underneath
and planes for Heathrow circle on the roof.
You'll find the body and all the air it exhales
smellier than by day; she's kinder, more supple.
Bend close to catch the delicacies of sleep,
to hear skin tick, to taste the mandragora
of night sweat. Lean forward and put a finger
on the spot you think the dream is.

Noah's Dove

It seemed the end of drizzling. Doves pair for life:
a tidy species to invite into the ark.
Men have no wings, no, not even Noah

so when the rain stopped he sought out the birds.
An old raven went first, wheeled around the dark sky
half the day just for kicks. He looped the loop, then hid

behind a cloud, only to return with no damned news
at all. A dove stops searching once she's felt the beak
of her first mate in the soft feathers of her neck.

Hopeless at distances, not used to questing,
she was sent out next, after the raven,
on the mission of her life. She went three times

the last time for good, en route to her own rainbow.
She left her mate the only single soul aboard,
trying to think of ways to spawn himself.

Mrs Noah: Taken after the Flood

I can't sit still these days. The ocean
is only memory, and my memory as fluttery
as a lost dove. Now the real sea beats
inside me, here, where I'd press fur and feathers
if I could. I'm middle-aged and plump.
Back on dry land I shouldn't think these things:
big paws which idly turn to bat the air,
my face by his ribs and the purr which ripples
through the boards of the afterdeck,
the roar—even at a distance—ringing in my bones,
the rough tongue, the claws, the little bites,
the crude taste of his mane. If you touched my lips
with salt water I would tell you such words,
words to crack the sky and launch the ark again.

Life

My life as a bat
is for hearing
the world.

If I pitch it right
I can hear
just where you are.

If I pitch it right
I can hear inside your body:
the state of your health,

and more, I can hear
into your mind.
Bat death is not listening.

My life as a frog
is for touching
other things.

I'm very moist
so I don't get stuck
in the water.

I'm very moist
so I can cling
onto your back

for three days
and nights.
Frog death is separation.

My life as an iguana
is for tasting
everything.

My tongue is very fast
because the flavour
of the air is so subtle.

It's long enough
to surprise
the smallest piece of you

from extremely
far away.
Iguana death is a closed mouth.

Rattlesnake

My rattlesnake has warm skin.
He sleeps by my feet and rustles
through my dreams, his diamond
back glistening all night.

Better than a fat alarm clock
is his subtle rattle at seven,
his cool glide towards breakfast,
his little fangs clinking the tea cup.

Cabbage Dreams

After dark, cabbages are proud and brilliant,
supercool. We stalk the garden
under the moon discussing politics with flowers.
We inspect your houses in the early hours
criticising the curtains, wondering about
the furniture, amazed at your reading habits.
Your clothes baffle us though we know
about layers and the colour of leaves.
We stare at your flabby fingers while
you sleep, speculate about your hairstyles.
Daytimes we fall back into ourselves,
sit around in vegetable racks, clutch
stubby leaves round our green shoulders
and hope you remember our sweet hearts.

Pig

You think of me
as clean and tasty,
don't want to know
about the mud, the tail,
the terrible trotters

don't want to know
about the neat little hats
in my wardrobe, the orchid
collection and the lengths and lengths
of breaststroke, the days and nights
in the Railtrack buffet
and the mad rapture for molluscs.

Hedgehog

The road is slick
in the rain
and good slugs
can be nuzzled
out of shadows
under hedgerows.

I understand.

It's plain
you can't hurry across
even when those other lights
come at you
preceding
the hurtling mountain.

Rhinoceros

What else to do
with the rhinoceros inside me
but feed him up with good hay,

cream his rough hide
with almond oil
until it gleams,

polish the two horns
on his face
with beeswax,

rinse his scaly feet
in rosewater,
once prepared

let him find the deepest pit
of mud inside my heart
and let him roll, roll, roll.

Elephant Woman

Nothing left except to grow
into my elephant skin,
expand into the great folds,

unfurl my ears across the kitchen,
remove myself into the bathroom
for nine days to celebrate my nose

and with my generous feet
tread gingerly round the house.

The Mad Cow in Space

Down there is little England, London, a dose
of crazy vision showing me a row
of heads on spikes outside the Tower. Still rotten,
still beautiful but ruined for me, now
I've seen stars with no atmosphere in the way.
Millions are on the Underground, going to work.
I can see them too, teeming just under
the Earth's crust. I'm weightless. Couldn't
fall over if you pushed me for a year.
The silence is an uproar and I write
with a special pen in which the ink can flow
without gravity to drag it to the page.
I'm trying to escape the pull myself:
don't want to look back at the Earth or send
more messages down to base about the way
it looks from here. Believe me, every smash,
every shot, every crack and blast is visible
and going right to plan but I can't stand
the Earth's screams as the blood touches her prissy skirt.

The Mad Cow is a Vogue Model

Giovanni, trained in Paris, has now spent
twenty-three minutes making me up.
Never before have I shown my whole body,
the full length of my combed-out tail, the visible
panty line, the unfurled rump to you,
my public. The photographer has planted me
in deep white space with perspective muddled on purpose.
I can't stand up straight. He doesn't understand
that I fall over sometimes and, anyway,
leaning is natural. But this is Vogue
where the upright and obedient send out
for anything they like. The Statue of Liberty
might do better. She is over three-
hundred feet high from torch to foundation.
Made of copper sheets beaten out by hand,
her first name was Liberty Enlightening the World.
She stands up straight without trying, but then
four gigantic steel supports run through her body.
And what will be at stake in this photo?
It's not an explicit language, but look
how I am snarling at the photographer.
I am snarling at his lens and through it a world
which wants my teeth, my eyes, my taste—and not
these words, these little deaths, these individual
devils, these visions of the whole damned lot.

Cheetah Run

I whisper, 'I'm coming baby,' to the distant hare
though my head's turned the full 180° away.
'Wait for me, no, run,' I shout because
I don't know which is more exciting, until
I'm accelerating into the full blast
of hare scent, grinning helplessly in the flood of it,
feeling my claws extend. My muscles
tug at me, and the tufts and tangles of longer
hair where my limbs join the torso.
Going after it like this, maybe I'd look more polite
if I kept my eyes on my own twitchy paws
or anywhere but where they want to go
towards the fine-tuned smell, the crunch of bone,
the blood at last as I turn to see his pain.

Drafts

The wind must be blowing
at Gale Force Ten. I have to lean
just to stay upright.
Either this gust

can shout louder than me
or it's made my own words fall
up into the air.
Perhaps I'll follow.

Northern Lights

We watched the islands from the waterfront
as though they held a clue to what was next.
The wind built up in gusts to match our hearts
and blew the café chairs into the water.

Police in boats fished out the furniture
with poles, making us laugh until the chuckles
rolled through us like the whale's back
rolls through water, like the islands

stretch through the north seas. I have stolen
some of the light which drenches you this midnight
to wish you all the islands in the world
and every one a different kind of peace.

Mandrake Pie

At home and abroad, we English brag about pie.
Our sailors bring home not just those heart-shaped boxes
crusted with little shells, but pie-cutters carved in doldrum days.

Implements of bone, one, two, or fabulously three-wheeled,
but always true, they allow fancy lattice-cutting back home
where no girl is marriageable until her pastry is so translucent

a sailor can read his tabloid right through it. Mandrake,
smelly, dangerous root of wonderful virtues, makes
the queen of pies, gives women babies and holds the wisdom

of the screaming dead. Pull your mandrake at dawn, double root
said to have grown from seeds of murderers put to death.
Ignore the shrieks as you tug and the scent that turns you on.

Bake it in the hottest oven you can get to make the air expand,
the pastry rise, as light as babies' breath. Ease the dough
into the tin, fill to the brim with the rough-chopped root,

and sprinkle with milk and water. Cover with pastry; seal
with a fork and then, and only then, may you lightly prick
the surface of your pie all over to let the screams escape.

A Visit from Janey

Janey wants to wreck my bathroom she's
so out of it. She's staggering towards
the unexpected wall of glass, waving
her bottle of booze, she's raiding the cabinet
for pills and screaming at the lime-scale stains
in the bath. The echo suits her voice so she smiles
and sits with a bump on the wooden toilet seat,
then grins up at the overhead cistern,
as she slips her beaded dress over her head.
So here's her stocky body, her small girl shape
slumped and naked on my toilet.
And now she's resonating my white tiles,
vibrating my roomy old bath: 'O Lord,'
she croons to the lime scale, 'O Lord,' to the tap
which drips, 'O Lord,' to the overhead cistern,
cold porcelain, on which is gathering
the magic condensation of her breath.

Brünhilde

Brünhilde is not a young
woman. She is as old as
God and much heavier. I
am vanquished by her purple
quilted slippers, the way a
whiff of boiled kidney slips from
both the insoles when she walks.
I want to drink out of them,
a good strong rioja with
its own tang set off by hers.
She doesn't insert curlers
but I intend to make her.
They must all be dusty pink:
many of the little prongs
must be worn away or snipped
off leaving small prickly nubs
that catch at my skin when I
nibble her ear. O but her
perfume must be old piss and
Pledge, and I will be her dog,
wear her stiff nylon housecoat;
Brünhilde with her penchant
for Silk Cut, the French poems of
Rilke, her instinct for the
most vivid ways to ripen,
the most vivid ways to rot.

Watching Medusa

Struck dumb when I saw
her scalp begin to stir,

saw the little eyes slide
like drops through her hair,

saw them look back at me
kindly and fluid

as a bunch of lovers.
I cannot speak or move

in case I do wrong to her and
close the sweet hissing mouths.

To Rotterdam for the Rosie B. Babes

Even the children are dancing and in the foyer
of the nightclub the ornamental fish are restless.
I've been ten hours getting to Rotterdam
but Rose on tenor sax gives it some throat
as specialist dancers turn out in black and white
for some low-slung, loose-kneed jiving. We drink Grolsch
for free because my sweetie knows the barman.
Rose says, 'I've been singing that song for twenty years
and still don't know what it means.' Well I can tell her.
It means lights on in Rotterdam and shine
on the grubby buildings, the ferocious port.
It means Rose, two saxes, trumpet, and trombone,
piano, traps and bass, all peeling back
layers of occupation, layers of blitz;
Rose folding sea walls and reclaimed land,
rolling up canals. It means the North Sea
swallowing the whole damned lot as Rosie
sings again *My Funny Valentine.*

Framed

She enters the movie from nowhere as all stars do,
to lean against the rail, dab the fuschia towel
with the palm of her little hand to dry the sweat.
Behind her, the salmon-pink double garage door
starts to open outwards and we hear
the rumble of a glossy car. She turns,
and her cheekbone cuts an arc against the sky.
Her eyes pan up and our shot follows them,
up, up the planted hill, past the blue roofs
the needle firs and the unreal palms, past the cacti
and the pink blossoms, past the skyline sun
and the few words of script behind a cloud,
to the corner of bare canvas right above her
which proves the sky is always the wrong way round.

Les Roses

after Rilke

I

If sometimes you're surprised
by my coolness
it's because inside myself,
petal against petal, I'm asleep.

I've been completely awake while my heart
dozed, for who knows how long,
speaking aphids and bees to you in silence,
speaking English through a French mouth.

II

You see me as half-open,
a book whose pages
can be turned by the wind
then read with your eyes closed;

butterflies stream out,
stunned to discover
they think just like you,
dab wings all over your face.

III

I'm an imperfect thing:
neat, layered
but spilling petals and pollen,
dropping bruised scent

on to the ground.
Essence of roses is not sweet,
but brown at the edges
like the air you breathe.

IV

So you think you caused
the bud to bloom,
enchanted the petals
into smiling.

We're talking Rosa Centifolia,
the hundred-petalled rose;
ask the bee, who can't concentrate
on anything else.

V

Space folds against space,
petal touches petal;
you look at me
as though you want to fall in,

make the flower
glow with your own image,
change my meaning
from rose to Narcissus.

VI

One rose is every rose,
so you say, just as one word
might be any other:
sepal, stigma, filament, fuck.

But then we can't speak floriculture,
can't discuss botany at all,
not even mention plant entropy
or the taxonomy of roses.

VII

O I'm leaning
against your forehead,
against your eyelid,
scenting your skin

with my own,
making you think
you can sleep
inside my face.

VIII

In my dream I could perform
water acrobatics
and swim with a troupe:
we leaned inwards

to form a perfect rose
which was, I swear,
a dead-ringer for the pattern
in your left iris.

IX

Now you've made
a saint out of me,
Saint Rose, open-handed,
she who smells of God naked.

But, for myself, I've learned
to love the whiff of mildew
because though not Eve, exactly,
yes, I stink of the Fall.

XI

You're inclined to confuse
me with yourself
as if you'd found
a mirror to worship.

I'm guilty too,
breathing you in
to catch a trace
of twice-blooming damask.

XII

Look, I'm growing
out of your left eye, snagging
your retina with little thorns,
rooting behind your frontal lobes.

What can you see
through the hundred pink tongues,
now you've a pupil who speaks
perfume, attracts bees?

XIII

You ask if I'm best friends
with the present, or whether
it's memory I nestle up to.
All the while you fill your mind

with pictures of me: happy,
thirsty, my petals as shrouds,
as pot-pourri on the bathroom shelf.
You try to read me aloud when you're alone.

XIV

Summer: for a few days
you lay around with us
breathed in pollen,
counted aphids,

watched us drop
one by one on to the path
where the scent
was especially heady.

XX

I can't turn a smell
into a single word;
you've no right
to ask. Warmth
coaxes rose fragrance
from the underside of petals.

The oils meet air:
rhodinol is old rose;
geraniol, like geranium;
nerol is my essence
of magnolia; eugenol,
a touch of cloves.

XXI

Spinning in the wind
so fast even the thrips,
my little petal-scarring insects,
fly off dizzy, so fast

you can't touch me
without risking a thorn,
can only watch as my heart
is shaken out into the world.

Parsnip Cardiology

Every Christmas, he buys parsnips.
Parsnips for roasting, loads of them, suddenly;
for boiling to mash with the mash; for flinging

into the turkey stock; for glowing creamy pale in the dark;
for somehow being always cold to his touch when raw;
for peeling noisily and crunching hard against the knife;

for staining once in the air; for being a member of the
carrot family, but sweeter; for being mud specked and wrinkled
and sprouting hair roots, yet altogether sound, with a core straight

through. But he may not be like that, after all, tomorrow
when they listen to his blood, listen for the flaw
in the valve that might stop his heart too soon.

Lovebirds

So she moved into the hospital the last nine days
to tend him with little strokes and murmurs
as he sank into the sheets. Nurse
set out a low bed for her, night-times, next to his.
He nuzzled up to her as she brushed
away the multiplying cells with a sigh,
was glad as she ignored the many
effluents and the tang of death. The second
last morning of his life he opened
his eyes, saying, 'I can't wake up'
but wouldn't close them for his nap
until he was sure she was there.
Later he moved quietly to deeper sleep,
as Professor said he would, still listening
to her twittering on and on until the last.

When I Died

I'm coming back on All Saints' Day
for your olives, old peanuts and dodgy sherry,
dirty dancing. I'll cross-dress at last
pirouette and flash, act pissed.
You'll have to look for me hard:
search for my bones in the crowd.
Or lay a pint and a pie on my grave to tempt me out
and a trail of marigolds back to the flat,
where you'll leave the door ajar
and the cushions plumped in my old armchair.

Professional Mourner

First I'll shave my head and take the phone off the hook.
I'll be close to madness so be sure not to speak
to me in case I infect you with crazy talk.
Fireworks, pipers and the mixing desk, all extra,
but loud, really loud, lamentation is basic.
Once excessive crying turned me blind for two whole days.
If you prefer I can be more silent, even,
than the dear departed: watch me speak in the sign-
language of the dead, catching my tears in muslin
nets before they crash to the floor. The job's diverse:
for you I'll kill a mouse, flay it and tap dance
with its little pelt around the open grave.
Please don't mind when I fling shit about, hurl insults,
copulate with granddad, molest your sister,
glue my crotch to your leg and drink the coffin dry.
'I am drunk! I am an animal!' I'll cry
as I steal the body, try to ransom it, take off
my skin and drape it over the coffin. Last seen,
riff-backing up the aisle in just my bones.

Spaghetti Junction

after Hans Magnus Enzensberger

Ranting, belted up and bitter, if it's not the leather heated
seats, it's the stonking space frame chassis, the abuse overtaking
and all that knowing about insurance, scarce spare parts,
then the traffic jam, the blue light, the stretcher.

From below you're watching instruments wink, you're slanting
under the alternative light of the anaesthetic.
The sister's uniform is white; she's well into her TV. Headphones.
Dramas you can't hear flicker over her dark face.

A gear crunches in the brain. Rear-view mirror,
signal, manoeuvre but don't look now. Central locking.
Even screaming hurts. Little bubbles rise,
glass marbles, in the intravenous drip.

The traffic clears; you're really motoring. The double
wishbone independent suspension's a tad spongy but then
spring rates, bushing stiffnesses and geometrics equal
roadholding fantastic. Everything's stereo, the drumroll,

stereo, heartbeat, the hiss of oxy-acetylene
cutting the ditched wreck open in blue, the pat, pat
of mud falling later, falling from the spade splat on
that place between cracked eyes where your spectacles once sat.

Motherland

after Tsvetaëva

Language is impossible
in a country like this. Even
the dictionary laughs when I look up
'England', 'Motherland', 'Home'.

It insists on falling open instead
three times out of the nine I try it
at the word Distance. *Degree*
of remoteness, interval of space.

Distance: the word is ingrained like pain.
So much for England and so much
for my future to walk into the horizon
carrying distance in a broken suitcase.

The dictionary is the only one
who talks to me now. Says, laughing,
'Come back HOME!' but takes me
further and further away into the cold stars.

I am blue, bluer than water
I am nothing, while all I do
is waste syllables this way.

England. It hurts my lips to shape
the word. This country makes me say
too many things I can't say. Home
of me, myself, my motherland.

A Letter to Dennis

Deep in the strangest pits in England, deep
in the strangest forest, my grandfathers
and yours coughed out their silicotic lungs.
Silicosis. England. Land of phlegm
and stereophonic gobbing, whose last pearls
of sputum on the lips, whose boils and tropes
and hallucinations are making me sick.

The point is how to find a use for fury,
as you have taught, old father,
my old butt, wherever you are.
Still rude, I hope, still raucous and rejoicing
in the most painful erection in heaven
which rises through its carapace of sores
and cracking skin to sing in English.

You are as live to me as the tongue
in my mouth, as the complicated shame
of Englishness. Would you call me lass?
Would you heave up any stars for my crown?

OXFORD POETS

Fleur Adcock
Moniza Alvi
Joseph Brodsky
Basil Bunting
Tessa Rose Chester
Daniela Crăsnaru
Greg Delanty
Michael Donaghy
Keith Douglas
Antony Dunn
D. J. Enright
Roy Fisher
Ida Affleck Graves
Ivor Gurney
Gwen Harwood
Anthony Hecht
Zbigniew Herbert
Tobias Hill
Thomas Kinsella
Brad Leithauser
Jamie McKendrick

Sean O'Brien
Alice Oswald
Peter Porter
Craig Raine
Zsuzsa Rakovszky
Christopher Reid
Stephen Romer
Eva Salzman
Carole Satyamurti
Peter Scupham
Jo Shapcott
Penelope Shuttle
Goran Simić
Anne Stevenson
George Szirtes
Grete Tartler
Edward Thomas
Charles Tomlinson
Marina Tsvetaeva
Chris Wallace-Crabbe
Hugo Williams